SOMEWHERE, A FIRE

DONNA KANE

HAGIOS
PRESS

COPYRIGHT © 2004 DONNA KANE

National Library of Canada
Cataloguing in Publication

Kane, Donna, 1959-
  Somewhere, a fire / Donna Kane.

Poems.
ISBN 0-9682256-8-3

  I. Title.

PS8621.A54S64 2004   C811'.6   C2004-901570-2

Printed and bound in Canada

The publishers gratefully acknowledge the assistance of the Saskatchewan Arts Board.

HAGIOS PRESS
Box 33024 Cathedral PO
Regina SK   S4T 7X2

ACKNOWLEDGEMENTS

Some of these poems have appeared, sometimes in slightly different versions, in *The Canadian Journal of Contemporary Literary Stuff*, *Descant*, *Event*, *The Fiddlehead*, *Grain*, *The Malahat Review*, *Other Voices*, and *The Wascana Review*.

I am grateful to Emilie Mattson, Barry McKinnon, and Clea Ainsworth, friends in writing and art; to Sheila Peters, Kim Goodliffe, and Jeanette Lynes for their readings of many of these poems; and to George Sipos for his friendship and for his tireless and meticulous editing.

I am grateful also to the Northern Lights College Foundation, and the late Paul Dampier in particular; to Patrick Lane and the Canada Council for the Arts Quest Program; to the Wired Writing Program at the Banff Centre for the Arts; to the Sage Hill Writing experience; to Mark Hanen for his early encouragement; and to Paul Wilson and Hagios Press.

Judith Krause made the final editing of this manuscript an enjoyable and rewarding experience.

To my family, especially Larry, Jason, and
Megan, for their patience and support.

CONTENTS

ONE

TWO

THREE

FOUR

If coincidence has a law
it's lonely

Karen Solie
"Action at a Distance"

ONE

LISTENING TO PATSY CLINE

Two untwined hay bales left in the field
play checkers into the spring. *King me,* they say.
A stalemate of chaff and snow. *King me.* Say,
let's hold to this original intention. Not fold
to *Oh cinnamon roll mouth. Kiss me.*
It's true. I'm listening to Patsy Cline
and it's affecting my good taste, my respect
for things unsentimental, but pick
even one of Patsy's songs
and tell me she doesn't flatten your heart
like a penny on the track, turn your smallest absence
into a train whistle longing up the banks of the river
through poplar forests, across fields of stubble
to Red Deer, Regina, the Trans Canada Highway,
a furrow of hurt so long, so deep, it's not true
I'm happy. But how to deny it.

THEY DON'T

Things don't vanish into thin air, they don't.
In a city far from home the morning leans
into a scorcher, haze burning off twenty years into a pasture light
thinning the brick buildings, the amphitheatre turrets. Up the
  street
a tuba moans, only the slim window remains a stiff blade
of dark. I don't want you to go. Light slants
under the moth-gray planks of a calf shed in spring.
Bright on straw beds indented by cows long gone to pasture.
Just one more minute, I say. Just
one. Brome grass grows through manure, the lost calf
returns to the place it last nursed, the dark
green spears, a single blade drawn tight between my thumbs,
slit of window, my breath a sound the grass carried into the air.
Today things grow small. The river where I was born, a scar
I trace between your ribs, the curtain drawn,
the blade sound returning, here, of all places,
as if nothing had changed. Would ever.

SIGNS

In the country at night, you
are who the splayed stars,
the moon about to split its gut,
lift their glass to.

To your boots
grinding down the gravel, to your
heels squeaking nibs of snow.

The tab of your zipper clicks against your coat
loud as a misaligned jaw. Sight
a tooth knocked out. Your ear
a tongue
fixed on what's left.

Tonight it seems to be you.

So you imagine an expression of devotion
in the night sky, planets stopped mid-crunch
simply to dote on you, forgetting

for the moment your impatience
with Henry Harris who heard
the voice of the Lord
in a bulldozer's gears,

took it as a sign. Hasn't
let go.

WHIRLWIND

Who were you, the one I was talking to
when the dust devil exceeded our expectations,
gathered three-storey mass like cotton candy on a great
   twirling cone
at the fair, snapping animal balloons from ribbons,
sucking up tents, tables T-boned, their checkered cloths
and plates of fruit taking flight,
though my hat
never stirred from my head.

My own patch of ground still as an O
while all around me
the earth's debris parachuted upward
toward the voice of God, saying,
"What you thought was your life
is now something else." A whole tent
rising like the best-made kite, medusoid,
flexing, releasing, urging its body
toward heaven. I watched it

go. Leaving you,
a bit of cotton shirt and a baseball cap.
I grapple for a name, a name, my mind
scissoring toward your thud back to earth, a few feet east maybe,
disheveled, the consonants and vowels rejoining
into what can bring only disappointment,
having lost you for so long.

THIS RAIN

It's what I imagine of the tropics, this rain —
freakishly warm, monsoon heavy,
plunging through poplar,
roiling clay roads.

Who, living in the north, wouldn't want
to go out in it? Maybe the fawn wonders
what this has to do with mother; it too
struck dumb by the downpour, both of us
pinned to the field, so close
I might touch its ear.
If I did, we'd be more water
than flesh, our senses washed out, those
old connectors diverted,
our ability to be startled streaming away
in a flush of light.

RED PYJAMAS

When the magician aired his secrets
disappointment followed.
Though how many times I'd asked to know.

I just want to be left alone
to eat my lunch, to watch my red pyjamas flare
in the spoon's curve, my movements
loop and swerve; watch how when I flip the spoon
I switch directions like a balloon losing air,
some would say frantic
to shake off the burning flannel.

It's as if springtime wants it out with me.

Too impatient, I never came to anything.
No wisdom steeped, no great truth or calmness
revealed itself. Not once have I talked
to the dead.

WANT

I want to be a dry stone
baking after months of cold,
an element
turned *hi* by the sun.

To heat up and not make a move,
no questioning voice or shadow of intent,
to want nothing
but a black ant to skitter across my back,
to have it pick me, pick me
with equal indifference.

JACK-IN-THE-BOX

Light twitches its ear,
lifts its hackles

to garlic shoots
cracking bulbs in the fridge.

Spring a rolled Jeep plunked upright.
Shadows winched, their sleight-of-hand

casts mine up the road
lighter than a crepe paper hat.

Another year contracting.
Ice snaps along ditches,

pussy willows pop
their sockets. Blind

and agog, their little
engines revving.

TWO

ON WAKING TO SNOWFALL

1

Drew back the curtain and autumn blew its fuse,
a pull-chain expectation split by the leap-heart crack
of a snow-covered lawn and three angels caught in the snow.
And some dumb jerk's footprints tromping
across them, searing the earth,
while the angels walk away through the tips of their wings,
confirming something sad inside you, something forsaken,
the way you come upon an accident on a quiet highway
and almost hope for a death, the world going on
without you, the endless guessing
and the one thing else that happens.

2

The sun bright as the snap on Judy's shirt pocket,
the sky pulled to a rare thinness. On the deck
chimes shoot the breeze,
until someone unhooks them, carries them singing
toward the back shed where they awaken the dog
to a deer in the yard and the dog takes off barking,
the deer jerking its head, bounding through the trees
across the dirt road where Judy comes barreling
in her one-ton Ford, a cocoon of dust trailing,
the two of them striking
at the very same instant I lift my glass,
thinking the moment exquisite
and where's Judy heading so close to supper?

3

Something nags at the edge
of things. When I read,
it recognizes vowels,
syllables, tries to stir
into words. When I walk
past the store window,
it catches its reflection,
tries to hold me to it —
remember me? Dissolving
quiet as cumulus
on the brain's blue tongue.

4

The grasshopper
cinches in. In every leap
a leap. You never see
its husked mouth open
but you hear it   singing
in the field. Disembodied afternoon.
From the stand of barley the house so silent
I think it will explode. The path from its foundation
to my foot   a fuse.

5

Enter a room for the first time
in which someone has left your suitcase. Reach
for your socks and from your bent position
see the legs of a dresser. Stand up
thinking mirror but your reflection is a paneled wall.
Never have you felt more absent, more able
to focus on weather instead of your place in it.
The entrance cleated. The f-stop closing. Never
has the world seemed so cold. Its indifference more clear.

6

Familiar as our bedroom at night,
each washboard bend of the road memorized
like the bed's edge, each dip
a dresser reached for in the dark, nights
when I try not to wake you, our bodies moons
of remembered light. If I forget
to mention love, it's because I drove
not knowing if I'd stopped at the four-way,
if the lights were still on at Parker's, if memory alone
reaches toward you, too.

7

Ditches thick with sweet clover and willows
leafed out hide the mule deer. Its weight kicking in
as I pass. The rustle of leaves on hide, the sure thud
of hooves like swallowing something sweet
now I don't know what to long for.
The hunch borne out: I've come this far and the ditch has yet
to rise on its haunches, turn the foul breath
of whatever I can't imagine toward me.
Deer move into the field. The heart
hangs on to its secrets. As long as this seems true
I can convince myself of anything.

THREE

ON SEEING A FOX
WITH A DEAD GOPHER IN ITS MOUTH

How well the gopher played its part,
sagging sock, body draped, at your service, bones
small mallets sounding the scale
of ditch grass and willow. How well

it would have fallen
into the arms of John Cowan
in Grade 7 Drama.
My face to the wall.
Told to forget my muscles
on cue, to fall
with my back toward the boy who stole stickers
from the downtown Deli. Rolls of red decals
saying *boneless, reduced*. Plastered
to the breasts of pin-up girls
in other boy's lockers, and oh —
I just couldn't do it,
froze before I'd begun, and yet
today, that fox, that gopher.
I felt, like the silent swath of
the fox disappearing
through ripening wheat, death's comb
part the hairs on my arms and neck, felt
with a sureness and a
calm that surprised me,
its sudden ability to carry me over,
and in mine to be carried,
so swiftly, so indifferently,
through the terrible workings
of something like that.

DISHPAN HANDS

The Dash-8 plummets through clouds,
a piece of silverware flashing through suds.
As though God has been doing dishes and a fork has slipped
through his hands. Idly God fishes, groping the bottom
with his fingers, believing as he must, he'll know
each object by its touch, but the truth is, he's distracted, thinks,
there's gotta be more than this kitchen sink, thinks, I'd rather be
anywhere else but here, give me a window
with polka dot sheers, a built-in Maytag,
a three-day week, someone else
to answer their prayers.

FOUR WOMEN FROM ZELLERS

When I pass the four clerks
who meet each day to buy scratch-and-wins
and stand taking turns at the garbage bin (their tickets poised,
thumbnails itching), I have learned to grow quiet,
slow my gait, hold my breath while each turn
passes, to hear them laugh, say they never believed it anyway,
and especially here, 2:30 PM, shirts to re-pin,
chicken wings thawing on a counter at home.
"Last week I won five bucks," one might say,
and it wouldn't matter if I've heard it before
I'm prepared to hear it again. Oh I have lost so many things,
yet at every turn, through every door I still make that leap
into the heart's lost-and-found. In the opened drawer
closing I slam shut the deal
to throw away logic, to not say a word if all I have lost
could be waiting there.

PLAYING CARDS AT THE SENIORS HALL

Sometimes I can't forgive
God's utter lack of grace.
If I ask anything
it's to be given time to swallow,
a chance to meld,
not to die with my mouth
full of egg salad sandwich
the way Phoebe did last Friday —
all those cards held tight to her chest
turned face-up on the floor.
Don't think the bunch of us
didn't look —
playing into God
and Phoebe's perfect hand.

MORNING PRACTICE

Someone's in the dumpster. Every few seconds his ball cap
two-steps the rim, his hand flashes
an edge of glad-green, pooling the light
before dipping back down. Boys
with hockey gear pass by unnoticed.
A woman by a truck fishes for keys. Then.
The apocalyptic wail of a siren up-street. Everyone stops.
The man in the dumpster rising to look, the woman
faltering at her half-opened door. Boys against hockey sticks.
For a moment they are one, banded together, alpha and omega,
brothers and sisters, the galactic spin that draws them
into the hot ball centre that could change, if not the world,
at least the part that makes us lonely
until a boy hollers out, *There's a man in the dumpster!*
and the truck radio cuts loose Billy Graham mid-sentence,
his bravado bouncing off their passing deposit
on an all-for-one. The siren a nickel spinning its edge
before wobbling face down in the Coke-can swill of familiar
   disorder.

DOUBTING THE MOONWALK

Absence is a winter storm,
a two-lane highway bunched into one,
shoulders narrowed, snow bending
jack pines pinned mid-mantra —
           do you give? do you give?
In the north, we don't give
notice. Cold and lonely, we excuse
the largest departures, nights
when the moon burns holes
through our sleep, jerks
us awake to say *look* —
is this really a face with a footprint on it?
The belief of wherever we've been waning,
glory thinning in the long wait
for an encore. Only the bull moose
licking salt from the tracks seems full
of the moment, oblivious to the day's
come and go. Its slow whiting out.

THE MAN WITH A HAND TRANSPLANT

Some things you don't think about — the way a wasp
fits perfectly inside the ribcage of a mouse,
or how well your hand has been stitched to his wrist,
though it's not that either,
it's the way your fingernails grow quicker than his,
the clippers in his pocket a secret between you,
how the hairs on your knuckles are curly and red,
his own hair black
and poker-straight, how he's starting to wonder
where your hand has been, how each palm reads a different fate,
leaves another man's fingerprints on his bed,
how you spoon his sugar, sign his cheques
(crossing his Ts like never before).
When he snaps your fingers he's afraid you'll come,
and the household cat he's never liked
can't keep your hand from stroking its fur.

SAFETY MEASURES

On the return flight, seated once more
by the emergency door, given the same spiel:
pull the handle, lift the window, fling it
into what I imagine will be the open Pacific
or a timber forest, trees spearing metal,
framework bending, all of us screaming
for air and two feet on the ground.
This, after days with a man
who locks the house tight
when he's at home, unplugs the toaster
with no chance of a storm. I casually say it,
"Couldn't I just open that door any old time?"
The flight attendant looks confused, so I explain —
"Like pulling the fire alarm when there's no fire."
"Of course not," she says (I'm so relieved),
"unless you want the cabin to decompress."
And it's like I've breached a faith
that hadn't existed until that moment.

Because I'm sure it's all she's thinking,
my eyes keep straying to the exit sign,
my body ready to rise in slow motion:
pull out, lift up, push away. The entire flight,
peanuts and safety card gripped in my hand,
the entire flight, the seatbelt light left on.

SUNSET, JULY

A chip of orange light glitters
against the west side of a jack pine,
the sun's expanse
contracted to a single strip
on one patch of bark
deep within so many other pines.

Sleep burning quietly at the edge of my sheets.
I toe-nudge toward it, my drowsing mind a tissue
held just above a low-banked ember. If I could keep
my eye on the one most proximate thought
as it's drawn up the flue, kindling for the crossing,
and snatch it back,
a cell might resurrect. The thought,
and all I am of it, returned
to its waking moment, but more alert,
hair on end, struck
with a touch of the hereafter.

FOUR

TWO KNEES TOUCHING

Once, sitting at a table I touched knees
with an old friend; at first I wasn't aware of it,
then suddenly I was and didn't move my knee.
Neither did he move his.

If our conversation altered at all
it wasn't apparent.

So I never knew
if each thought the other was lost
in some preoccupation so that moving
would only clue us in to something
made suddenly awkward
or if each thought the other began it
until it seemed too late to make the change.

Even now I can't believe
how warm a knee can be,
how, years later, it's still
the thing I think of.

Not motive,
but the body's dumb insistence
on mouth finding mouth, hand holding hand.
Not confession. Just the heat
of two knees touching.

DRUNK, WE HELD THE SLOUGH IN OUR ARMS

You could say we paddled the slough badly,
while the canoe, feeling the tip
and tilt of our bodies,
refused to take part, grew moss,
hummed quietly to itself.

If there were clouds
I don't remember them
blocking the sun.

We weren't watching for signs.

We were friends
headed for disclosure, a full moon
displacing every other heart and pulse.

We weren't careful.

We didn't keep things to ourselves.

Shells, once coiled on the muddy bottom,
empty and crumble
in the warm spring air.

Stumbling home through the marsh
we were reckless to think
the best way through this
is headlong into it,
to reach the shore dry
means nothing.

All night I itch from the flush
of our undoing, dream
of leeches on my ankle,
algae between my toes,
shoes burning in the fire
while a bird I don't remember
sits alone on a branch, refusing
to listen.

MOUNT RUNDLE

The mountain keeps a stiff lip, its jaw pointed
toward clouds moving east. It's possible
the one shaped like a woman will reach you by evening.
Miles away, I divide and distill this emptiness. My cirrus hand
trailing the back of your neck, your breath
on my skin, the shape of it billowing
past tree line, past summit,
nimbus gathering nimbus
until the clouds burst open
and the mountain stares   as it were
at nothing.

THE BESSBOROUGH HALL

filled with a country and western two-step and men
with packs of smokes embossed through the rear pockets
of their wranglers, their western shirts with pearl snaps
and triangular insets of coloured cloth, their cowboy boots
and good Stetsons and a pure pulse inside them
that knows instinctively how to thrust you into the upbeat
like turning a newly sewn garment inside-out, poking out the
    corners
with something sure, a knitting needle maybe, poking that
    corner out
each time crisp and sharp — men who learned to dance
some other way than counting steps
or looking at their toes, who move
with dogfight confidence restrained men who listen to jazz
must surely envy, the way they propel their women
to something brighter than the shuffleboard wax
sprinkled on the floor before the lights go down

and you are led. The twang
of a steel guitar, a pointed boot urging you
to the spired summit, the height of a really good cry.

CONSPIRE

I can tell when someone's staring
the way I know the moon's waxing
with the blinds drawn. The feeling

you get when the toaster's about to
pop — the air bristling toward
spontaneous combustion.

Your stare is infrared.
Here's the question.

If I could be the dog
who pretends
not to see the cat
to keep itself from lunging
would you disappear?

Who knows how much we conspire, or why.

How much is a pike that lugs, for no reason at all,
its heavy and muscled heart
straight into the net.

VALENTINE

The Elvis teddy's singing heart fibrillates its body off
the shelf. "I'm all shook up," it seizures, guttural on the floor.
Whoever pushed its button is long gone. Last-minute
buyers step around him, their eyes on the mint-condition hearts
still shrink-wrapped, shimmering on the shelf. A boy
wants the oversized cardboard heart covered in velvet
with ten chocolates tucked inside.
"Do you think she likes you as much as you like her?"
his mother cautions and you could say she doesn't wish
to see him hurt and even you agree
a dollar a chocolate is too much to pay.
So why this sadness rising in defence
of a one-way love you'd never wish upon yourself
but which comes sure as Elvis
in a plush shag bear suit borking at your feet
and every aunt who said it wouldn't matter who,
he'd tire of you soon enough. Because.
The day's one good aim is its safety net. Those padded walls
that let you act out with a backup plan.
Let you give the rose and not really *mean* it.
Not only for your own saved face
but for that gawking audience of hearts
still throbbing.
Ritual no more than a gadget, a rusty can opener that slips
at the wrist's first turning.
Maybe not, thinks the boy,
setting the chocolates back on the shelf.

I SEE YOU IN THE DINING ROOM BELOW ME

I leaned over the balcony
and my heart twinned, split
like a pull 'n peel twizzler,
a double street lamp,
two bulbs glowing in opposite directions.
I wanted to do a pirouette,
a pike with a twist, to come
from five metres and not make a splash.

I flatter myself.
Pretending I could fall
head over heels
that gracefully.
Lungs catching air
like a pinwheel flashing
through an adolescent sun down
a hill without brakes but

it's a worried old song.
The needle pinning the groove
before starting to play,
the elevator dropping before reaching the top

and you
were bluffing all along,
       whispered *jump* in my ear,
your own to the ground, ready

for the tinkle of forks to bump the
glass stemware, the linen-topped table
glanced on descent, the rose carpet rising,
my mind reeling back for
a lap, a lap.

ALL OF LIFE THERE IS

> *Well, let's say this morning is all of life there is —*
> *Let's suppose the weather . . . the room . . . the*
> *bed . . . our cells . . . are it. . . .*
>
> Robert Bly

A hard winter, how close we'd come
to leaving, days in which I had never felt more
alone and you left me
lonelier still. Then — that day in April, the sun
melting the last of the snow and here and there
dandelion leaves cracking open the earth —
we stopped all of it to be giddy with spring.
For a moment it was all of life there was —
the highway, the ice cream,
the thirty-foot lumberjack sawn from a pine
we stopped to take a picture of. Couldn't the dogs,
(first a Doberman, then a Shepherd,
then a Rottweiler — I'm not kidding)
have turned up in someone else's Sunday drive?
The last one lunging at you
before lifting its leg on the chain-sawed boot
and I just couldn't stop laughing.
The dropped cone, the sun
melting it away like mad.

THE WAY YOU SLEEP

Each day you nap on the couch there's an increasing blankness
to it, as if your skull were wearing a hole
through your thoughts until it's a travesty
the way your body goes on without you,
each breath building into snort-stops and drools, a rhythm
you'll mimic later, laughing in the bar.
Truth is, you find it uncomfortable the way your body sleeps,
think, it's bad enough a child should fall, but an adult?
The view must be as good as dead — slack jaw,
shirt untucked, button hanging
by a thread. In a way, it's worse than death,
each time you rise, there's more to forgive,
until you'll be glad for the starched suit, the make-up, the
    rigor mortis
settling into formaldehyde, your grandmother's tired voice
saying how well you look, and wouldn't it be nice
never to wake up.

SURRENDER

On the roof, snow loosens its grip,
shoots down the tin, the sudden
noise of it filling me
like a spiked drink.

Before wit or my father's good
sense, before cup becomes
cup, twig
twig, I am on my own,
a simple sugar
with a flu-like ache.

Were it death coming at me,
or love, I'd dissolve
right into it
no complaint no naming.

I'd seek thrills
just to stay like this,
my weak knees blessing
and blessing again
that elegant pause
in which we drop.
Hands in air.

PLACE IS WHAT STANDS
BEHIND THE DOOR AND LISTENS

The disappointment of finding a field
out of country. The train that takes you somewhere
you've never been and still you find swaths, combines,
a tractor stopped for the mid-day break — you just know it —
or in evening, the field seeded, a cornfield
sutured between trees, gone gold, dusk
and the stalks still swell with dew.
Or the urge to take foreign things home, to pluck them
from their spot and put them in your hat or hang them
from your wall must be the fear
of never returning, anywhere,
to find your place again.

FOR GOOD

If I go away for a week, so much seems different.
The grass needs mowing, the cat, having disappeared for days,
returns hungry, grass stains on one paw. The peonies
have bloomed, it's rained an inch, the run-off
has marked the brick steps, and your father at the window
has stopped looking at the jays.

If I go away for a year, nothing will feel like news.
In ten, there will be even less to say.

I don't love you any more, but who can remember
when it actually ended, who can remember
the last time fog lifted from the pond, now frozen

the last time we left the restaurant we used to go each Friday,
the moment you leave any place you never thought
you would, but do.

THE STONE CATERPILLAR

On his bookcase, an ammonite,
thin enough to slip between finger and thumb,
macroaphalites . . . Middle Jurassic.
A stone caterpillar curled in my palm,
those long-ago passes at spirited boys, turned out badly.
How it could have begun with a Swallowtail, say,
or a Mourning Cloak caught in my upturned hand
and offered to my mother, to my sister Shannon, then
to the boy whose name I'd carved in the fence —
a small brown caterpillar, a velvet curl, the boy's lovely thumb
coming down hard, bursting
the seams of its plush tan jacket —
a peapod popping, death lifting its mouth
to blow   across the spot   exactly.

WALKING DOWN A ROAD, MUSING

The last thing I need
is another poem about a raven,
but this one chortles above my head.
And you think you've got something to say! I holler up
and it lets loose a feather, fluttering
otherly toward my bad mood.

Even you, who've seen it all
would be impressed at this, I bet.

What are the chances?
It drifts downward, slow as bliss,
and I'm starring in some commercial —
loose hair, T-shirt tight against my breasts,
upturned face exquisite, the feather
caught in my open hand,

the shaft's delicate curve, its
downy fluff ludicrously wimpy
for a raven, who, meanwhile, inside his clunky body
wrestles air, thrums through trees, squawks.

We've all got troubles.
We're all half-starved for a miracle.

FIVE

DRIVING, LISTENING TO HOLLY COLE

When the moose looms in front of your car
you're way past brake
already your mind has catapulted
off the hood, is thinking
ditch. On some nights death.
The tax note on your fridge
is gone, lodged inside a wedge of ear, a card trick
in the dark. The appointment you were heading for
a fizz of hoof and cleave and cartilage.
Your husband, a marble eye.
Your son, a spear of hair.
Alces alces, sings Holly Cole, *you are my dewlap of syncopation
my velvet bone, my even toe, my bell, my herbivore.*

WHO DOESN'T

for Larry

Who doesn't love a man
who can back a trailer
to within an inch of his mark,
who can read
not only the tracks
in the driveway but the payload
they carried, holds a finishing nail
in his mouth, a pencil behind his ear,
who studies the joists
of the unfinished building so thoroughly
you know you've disappeared
and for a minute
you are watching a boy
you haven't yet met —
his single-purposed concentration
so fierce it's clear
he loved the world before you
or any other girl came into it.

WAITING TO HEAR

Parallel worlds zip by me —
open the fridge and the salad dressing's expired
at an astonishing rate; in the studio,
a decade's worth of *National Geographics*
fill less than one shelf — pull back
and everything speeds up, zoom in
on one person, wait for his mouth
to say the word he refuses
and time slows
to the lengthening shadows
of late afternoon, a purplish hue
sinking into the cushions, a sweet
and bruised lament.

I'm so full of waiting
I may have outgrown you.
Now nothing you say
will be enough. A sonic boom
and I'm miles away, a dot
on the horizon, where simple things
assemble, grow beautiful, the snow,
the children shifting their feet
in the cold, keeping time to music
in a distant car, the lovers
walking away, their steps in sync
so their heads almost touch
then part, almost touch then part.

ECLIPSE, JANUARY 2000

What will be remembered:
the dead flies falling through my hair at the opened window?
My father's voice on the phone, "Are you watching?"
Tonight the beauty is in the moon's exactness,
a tooth anaesthetized, a feeling lost one shade at a time,
the way earlier, light drained from the sky,
a pearlescent ring around the horizon,
and the moon rose early
huge on the lip of the earth.
Fifty thousand years before the moon's this close again
and I don't want to make sense of it, don't want to be impressed
that in three hours it will eclipse itself, too.
The tricks are too many and arrive without argument — tonight
to the tune of *The National* and the voice of Peter Mansbridge,
my breath reduced to an obligation,
a litmus drawing felt in the dark: capillary — death
a moon my eyes never stray from.

"Has it started?" I ask my father, as if it were a sitcom,
as if it were *Frasier* and each shade a change of scene,
is Daphne, is Niles, is Roz, my father a fiction.

PHOTOGRAPH OF MY TWO CHILDREN
ON MOBERLY LAKE

for Jason and Megan

Paddles still snapped to their inflatable raft, my children float
lighter than a Pond Skater's slippery foot, a bead of oil
skimming a plate. Arms raised, they wave at the camera,
their bodies stilled as the beach behind them, its bleached line
a crease from hills unfolding their reflection.
Inside my children's opened hands
it's me they're holding. The shadow pressed into each palm
is my light leaving or about to enter. If I turn away,
their small hands close. Their arms lift higher
or fall into their laps. Their bodies drift closer or farther
from shore. Their mouths whisper *hello, goodbye.*

1964

while atomic bombs were discussed
I pushed toy tractors
and wagons through clumps of dirt
outside the kitchen window. Bunkers
below ground while yellow cubes of hay
and plastic chickens the size of thumbs
whose flimsy legs I bit in two. I'd had it
with chickens. Their constant tipping over.
All that non-stop pecking that never amounted to a thing
consumed. I wanted action — a dozen dirt holes
and a garden hose. My legless chickens
on the swim of their lives, pin feathers spinning
in the thrust and drown of a five-year-old heart.
Its unnamable urge toward reckless clouds.
Its own small sky.

HOME FOR CHRISTMAS

A string of coloured lights edge
the window frame. From my spot on the couch,
the yellow top left corner bulb tricks me
into thinking it's his headlights coming down the hill
though it's the wrong direction and too early,
but it flares like a match at the edge of my book,
catches my eye during the late news,
and every minute he doesn't arrive
burns brighter. Blinding the pages, my
fingers scorched. Words erupting
into flaming wrecks.

PERHAPS THIS IS WHY SOME JUMP SO EASILY

From twenty floors up the streets look benign —
the cars on Seymour so small and clean and waxed
you can taste their colours in your mouth —
the junkie and his hungry dog pass easily,
and every woman who rounds the corner could be you.
From here, a fridge falling from the back of a truck
seems a natural movement, and every woman who
crosses the street to buy a latte from the sidewalk café and
kisses the man who saves her a seat
could be you.

NEW YEAR'S EVE

Staring out the window, the cat sees something new.
When I look, it's the same as it's been for days,
the willow chair iced to the ground, arms curved
toward the frozen dugout, stiff blades of grass
knee-deep in last week's snow, trees stock-still.

A cat will believe anything,
thinks the season could change from winter to spring
at the opening of a door. Each blink of its eye
ending a world. A new one beginning, every time.

I start to count down, but my husband says
I've set the clock wrong. It's already past midnight.
I don't want to go forward. I want the door
to shut from the other side, but already
the future has slipped through the window,
drifts past us in sleep, blazes trails through the house
only it can see.

SPRING

The water is running, its sound
has elbow room for gladness, a pebble
inside a hubcap, bursting
over ditches, a melon split in two, rocking.

I've been landlocked for days, what's possible
collapsing into its opposite, a harangue
of blue notes.

This runoff could carry a meadow in its throat.

I've grown clumsy and carry little.
Yesterday — kitty litter, frozen peas, instant cappuccino
— you could see I needed a cart, how close
each word comes to its antonym:

What repels. What's holy.

This window I stare from,
looking west until I'm on east's
back door. The new moon
growing full, then
new again.

THAT SAID

Each word has a flat, a slow leak, a sun
pinking the dust-furred air, then gone.

It would be better to have just held you,
to have said *there are no words.*

Along the banks of the pond
frogs ascend from their deep sleep,

their voices lift out of the dusk, rise
like a ball toward a brief gloved light.

How surprised they are, how strange
thoughts sound uncoiled in the air.

Each consonant a carrot wedged from the clay,
its bright orange placed in our mouths.

Each vowel a star uncorking the dark, spilling
into words, sentences, awkward copulations of truth.

Once more I've made too much of things.
In time I'll think, too little.

I DREAMT MY GRANDFATHER WAS ALIVE AFTER ALL

and working at a second-hand store.
Perkier than before, he phoned, wondering
why I hadn't called. In the background
customers haggled over bits of wool
and a jar of buttons beside the till.
Slipping their knots, threads loosened in the air,
every button he ever wore poured into a pickle jar.
Small bones through a rain stick, those deadpan discs clattered
with the frayed edges of Monday's wash,
the pearl snap of his wrangler cuff, the corduroy button
of his coverall strap, rising from under cushions,
from cracks in the couch, the powdered plank floors
of the country hall, the linted pocket
of his favourite vest where his fingers fumbled
for a pinch of snuff before falling face down, jolting
me awake, the moon outside my window
a button on a tux.

LABOUR DAY WEEKEND AT THE LAKE

I wish, of course, for clear sky,
a heavy sun, the lake
to be a sheet of glass.
Instead, a dump of snow.

Fireworks, their fuses taped over,
have leaned in the closet so long I hope
for the wind to blow the clumps of snow
from the trees before more branches snap.

I can no more stop this
than I can stop my thongs from slapping my heels
with every step and not only that —
no matter how faint, how small these expectations grow
they harbour the same blunt sweetness
as all the ones before it. A marshmallow browned
in the fire, its crinkled shell slipped off like a seersucker cuff
and toasted again.

No matter how late,
somewhere, a fire being lit.

SNOWED IN

Snow fills ditches to a blue dip
sinks the stubble fields, says:
We'll hear nothing more of coincidence, not here or here or here
each fence post capped, each root sealed.
Sshhhh, it says, *There'll be no more references,*
no preambles to accompany love.
There are no connections but the ones you've made.
No rutted road, this heart, not full
of holes but filled with a weight so void of distraction
it sees only forward. Knows nothing
of where it's been.

RALENTIR

for Marilyn and Shelagh

Raking leaves under the bare branches of a brilliant fall sky,
Larry's power saw clearing ski trails in the distance,
I amused myself by heaving leaves
so they made the sound of the Mediterranean —
how the wind blew that day, salt spray in our faces
while eating lukewarm samosas. Now
the memory of raking leaves is months past,
my legs so sore the next day I could hardly move,
the way each language must use different muscles,
the mouth moving uniquely with each dialect,
so we might guess by the lines on our faces
the expressions we used, the ones
we didn't, the words we traveled to reach
our end — the checkerboard sign
that snapped us out of it. Syntax downed
like a cottonwood, the lifted earth
rushing toward us.
Every last window rolled up.

NOTES ON THE POEMS

The introductory quotation is from Karen Solie's collection, *Short Haul Engine* (London, ON: Brick Books, 2001).

The epigraph on page 45 is from Robert Bly's "Thinking About Old Jobs" in his collection, *Morning Poems* (New York: Harper Flamingo, 1998).

Donna Kane lives with her family near Dawson Creek, British Columbia, where she is active in the Peace River literary community as organizer and host of readings, festivals, and writing retreats. Her work has appeared in literary magazines across Canada. *Somewhere, a Fire* is her first book.

Somewhere, a Fire is set in Adobe Garamond, a typeface designed by Robert Slimbach, the roman based on the matrices of the Parisian typecutter Claude Garamond (1499-1561) and the italic on the work of Garamond's contemporary Robert Granjon (1513-1589). Garamond's letter forms, widely accepted in France and much of Europe, were influential in replacing the gothic or blackletter forms which were then the standard, and many of the most widely used typefaces in history are based on his designs. Robert Granjon's italics were among the first letterforms designed to harmonize with the roman rather than stand alone. The typeface was issued in digital form by Adobe in 1989.

This book was designed and typeset by Donald Ward, who also designed the cover.

The cover illustration is a photomontage of *The Glass House*, a mixed-media sculpture by Emilie Mattson.

Edited by Judith Krause.